# Smart Data

# Smart Data

Driving Innovation through
Strategic Intelligence

## Lloyd Corder, Ph.D.

CorCom, Inc.
Research & Consulting

Copyright © 2017 by Lloyd Corder, Ph.D.

All rights reserved. No part of this publication may be reproduced, distributed or translated in any form by any means, including photocopying, recording, or any other electronic or mechanical methods, without the prior written permission of the publisher, except in the case of a brief quotation embodied in critical reviews and certain other noncommercial uses permitted by copyright law. For permission requests, write to:

CorCom, Inc.
Gateway Towers, Suite 370
320 Ft. Duquesne Blvd.
Pittsburgh, PA 15222 USA
Tel: 412.201.2636  Fax: 412.201.2606
www.corcom-inc.com

SBN-13: 978-1545081020

Printed in the United States of America.

Copyediting, proofreading and design by Jessica Cohen and Kara Buggy. Cover design by Sabrina Amann-Ross.

This publication is designed to provide accurate and authoritative information in regard to the subject matter covered. It is sold with the understanding that the publisher is not engaged in rendering legal, accounting or other professional services. If legal advice or other expert assistance is required, the services of a competent professional should be sought.

-From a declaration of principles jointly adopted by a committee of the American Bar Association committee of publishers.

CorCom, Inc. books are printed on long-lasting acid-free paper. When it is available, we choose paper that has been manufactured by environmentally responsible processes. These may include using trees from sustainable forests, incorporating recycled paper, minimizing chlorine in bleaching or recycling the energy produced at the paper mill.

# DEDICATION

To Clinton Corder, M.D., Ph.D., my dad, who encouraged me throughout a lifetime to become more data-driven.

Little did I know that his help with grade school science projects, like building a fish-pole microbalance that was so sensitive it could weigh an eyelash, or spending time in his lab working on experiments would build my confidence and respect for data.

As an undergrad, he would encourage me to continue my studies and get a doctorate.

Throughout my career, he always wanted to hear about my research studies.

Then, when he started his own clinical research testing firm, I too found enough entrepreneurial courage to start my own marketing research and consulting firm.

Along the way, I eventually realized that he was always finding a way to say: "I love you and I'm proud of you."

# ACKNOWLEDGEMENTS

I've spent my career helping organizations build data-driven cultures, not because it's the latest fad, but because this philosophy works. Listing everyone who's supported me along the way would fill the entire book. I am grateful for their continued support. It's no slight thing.

During that time, I've had the immense pleasure of working with several thousand students at the Tepper School of Business at Carnegie Mellon University and the University of Pittsburgh as an adjunct professor. They've helped me continue to find ways to articulate the basic ideas of this book and communicate them in a way that was interesting, or at least kept them awake in class.

Finally, a special thanks to my friends and clients, who helped me conceptualize and refine this book. Hank Rettger, with his dry sense of humor and banter convinced me that what I had to say would be best shared with as many others as I could find who would listen. John Suttle reminded me to "delegate" some of the work by piecing together a few of the ideas I've been writing about in recent years. Chris Westphal helped me hone my key messages.

# CONTENTS

| | |
|---|---:|
| Introduction: Bill Miller | i |
| Big Data Is Not Your Sugar Daddy! | 1 |
| Step 1:<br>Start with People, Not Systems | 7 |
| Step 2:<br>Simplify Your Opportunities by Using the Improvement Formula | 11 |
| Step 3:<br>Realize You're Fighting a Battle of Perceptions | 15 |
| Step 4:<br>Be Clear about What You Want | 21 |
| Step 5:<br>Use Addition, Accounting and Attitude Measures | 25 |
| Step 6:<br>Setup Your Data Correctly in a Spreadsheet You Can Analyze | 31 |
| Step 7:<br>Keep Your Findings Simple, Very Simple | 35 |
| Step 8:<br>Analyze Your Audience | 43 |
| Step 9:<br>Tell a Story to Make Your Data More Interesting and Usable | 47 |
| Step 10:<br>Use a Snowman to Organize Your Meeting | 53 |
| *Summary of* Smart Data: 10 Steps for Making Better, Faster Business Decisions | 57 |

# BIG DATA IS NOT YOUR SUGAR DADDY!

That was the working title of this book before I tested it and found that twice as many people liked "Smart Data," so I changed it. What's the point of being data-driven if you don't use what you find?

Big data is hot right now. And some people act like big data will do all sorts of stuff they couldn't do before they started buying new software and finding golden nuggets in the millions of customer records, social media posts and other information sources they had laying around. It may well do that. However, this book focuses on a different part of the equation: Your people.

My question is simple: How much better could your organization be if it was more data-driven?

I'm not talking about just numbers here. A lot of organizations say they have a data-driven culture. They have piles of financials, endless lists of performance metrics and even results from the occasional surveys. Some of them even have "analysts" who wrestle with "big data" and come up with information about whatever numbers they were asked to crunch. But all that data doesn't necessarily translate into better focus, improved efficiency and increased profit.

What I'm talking about is a management philosophy, a way of thinking. Does your organization systematically improve, because your people understand the persuasive power of data? Do they quickly focus on what you need to know, gather the best information available, analyze it quickly and communicate what they learned in a way that wins the right hearts and minds? Are people encouraged to think like scientists who make decisions based on data?

A data-driven culture isn't about the minutia. Rather, it's more about the important stuff, the big picture. On the decisions that really matter, it means taking a disciplined approach by using data that's collected, analyzed and presented effectively so those decisions are more obvious and easier to make.

Not long ago, I helped run focus groups to test some proposed controversial health insurance advertisements that said if you bought insurance from the wrong company, you would be out-of-network (not covered) at the best hospitals in the area. One ad idea had a diver in half of a shark tank, while the other showed a beekeeper in half a bee suit, both very dangerous situations. The idea was that the diver and beekeeper—by not being properly protected—were taking on unnecessary risk.

Consumers in the sessions went ballistic.

They thought the ads were terrible and didn't reflect what they expected from a leading health care provider.

The feedback was so bad, the ads were scrapped. After the session, my client told me I just saved them $750,000 in development cost, plus their media buy, plus all the problems the ads would have created.

The focus groups—or data—helped clearly show the ads wouldn't work. Instead of guessing, debating or listening to the strongest advocate for the ads from inside the company, the consumers' voices were heard.

## The Five Top Benefits of a Data-driven Culture

At this point, you may be asking, "What's in it for me?" The answer: A lot. These are a few thought-starters.

*1. Jumpstart Your Organization*

Time is of the essence. Data helps you quickly guide and transform your organization, but not if you're waiting too long for insights and guidance you wish you had last week.

The purpose of this guide is to help more of your staff think and work from a data-driven mindset.

*2. Being Better Today than You Were Yesterday*

It's about your culture. Is your staff so committed to using data in their day-to-day operations, that they are constantly finding ways to get better, faster and more focused without you constantly nagging them? If not, what's holding them back? Instead of you pushing them, would it be better if everyone was pushing you? This is the essence of a good team, when individuals throughout the organization develop logical proposals, feel open to present their recommendations and push the organization to adopt them.

*3. Creating a Process, Not an Event*

A humming data-driven culture is more about a "process" and less about an "event."

A process is about the rate and velocity to which your organization is getting better. An event is about doing something one time or doing it only periodically, then sliding back into what's comfortable.

A data-driven culture is not for the faint of heart. It takes hard work, precision and dedication. Building a data-driven culture is not the "flavor of the month" management activity that employees quickly learn to give lip service to and tolerate for a while before something else comes along.

## 4. *Being Organized to Deliver*

Does your staff know how their performance impacts (improves or hinders) the service your customers demand and expect?

This is about self-awareness, knowing with certainty that specific behaviors lead to valuable results. Of course, this self-awareness is a whole lot easier to attain if your staff has the basic skills to effectively collect, analyze and present the data that helps manage this process.

## 5. *Making "Tough Sells" Easier*

Most senior leaders have learned that dictatorships don't work. It's a whole lot easier when people come to their own conclusions and are self-motivated to do something.

A data-driven culture helps get other leaders, cross-functional areas and decision-makers on board faster, with less resistance and more enthusiasm.

But that's not enough. The real value comes from understanding what other groups (customers, shareholders, etc.) really want. When you make key decisions based on what they value, your chances of winning go up, way up.

## What's in the Rest of this Guide?

The 10 basic steps you'll need to build a stronger data-driven culture. I love theory, but there's not much use for it here. We need to keep it simple, because building a data-driven culture is a topic that can very easily be overcomplicated and screwed up.

I'd rather offer concrete steps that I've already tested

and proven to work. Thanks to dozens of clients who have supported my work and thousands of individuals who have attended my classes or seminars, the basic process is already worked out.

Instead of offering hundreds of pages of techniques, my goal in this guide is to provide a strategic framework to help get you started and move more of your organization forward. Once you start, you won't want to turn back.

There are two audiences for this book: management and professional staff. For management, this book is about the philosophy of becoming data-driven, the key ideas, techniques and process that get you from where you are today to where you would like to be tomorrow.

For the professional staff, the book is a simple how-to guide. I've outlined some simple ways to think about data, what to look for, how to organize it, package it and present it to others (like management) so that everyone can make better decisions faster.

Lloyd Corder, Ph.D.

# STEP 1

## START WITH PEOPLE, NOT SYSTEMS

People—not systems—need to be data-driven. Some people think the best way to get there is to purchase an expensive software package or build an elaborate process. That's not what I'm talking about here.

The objective should be to help your staff develop a basic understanding of what it means to be data-driven and how they might get started with it.

An easy way to think about this is to consider the individual skills of the people on your team. Everyone has a set of "technical" (their area of expertise, skills, talents, etc.) and "soft" (communication, presentation, listening, etc.) skills.

Some are much better at one or the other. For example, most engineers become engineers because they gravitate to the technical areas and may have to work exceptionally hard to overcome shyness or breaking down their ideas into bit-sized chucks that other decision-makers can understand.

Generally, the more these technical and soft skills overlap, the stronger the employee. As I like to ask my students, "What do you call an engineer who is good at selling and presenting?" The answer: CEO.

Here's a visual diagram of what I'm suggesting:

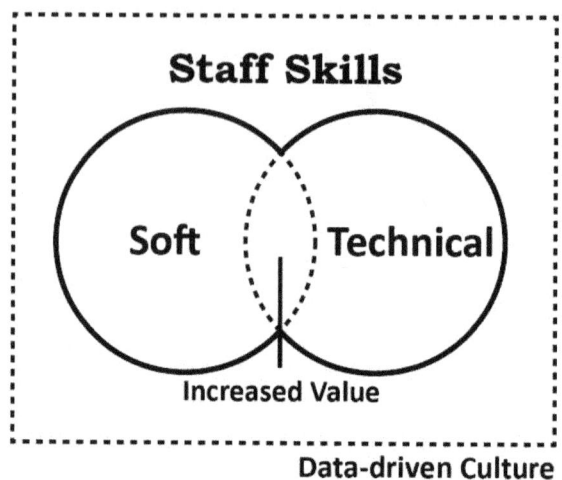

When you encourage a data-driven culture around each employee, it helps improve both the technical and soft skills of that employee.

Instead of a technical person saying, "Here's my data dump on my 50 slides that show you every intricacy," they take more user-friendly approaches, like telling an interesting story or showing a diagram to better show the impact of what they found.

Not long ago, I helped a software company train several hundred engineers, many of them had Ph.Ds. and were exceptionally strong technically. Through practice presentations, we looked for ways to make their entire pitches more persuasive and effective.

One of the presenters started his technical talk about wind forces and stress on airplane wings with a picture of a crash site. He asked, "Does anyone know what plane this is and how many people were killed in this accident?"

After a few guesses, he told them, "This is why we are here today. So this doesn't happen to one of your planes." You could have heard a pin drop.

For employees who are stronger at the soft skills, being data-driven helps them become more technical and persuasive.

I like to tell my students that marketers who are quantitative and comfortable with all kinds of data increase their stature and credibility. They start being perceived more like the financial staff, because they back up their beautifully presented and articulated points with data.

So, what I'm suggesting is that you encourage all of your staff to be more data-driven—not only in how they find, collect and analyze that data, but in how they boil it down and present it so the big decisions in your organization are easier to make.

Lloyd Corder, Ph.D.

# STEP 2

# SIMPLIFY YOUR OPPORTUNITIES BY USING THE IMPROVEMENT FORMULA

Several years ago when my friend, Clark Walter, wrote three words on a white board, "Present-Future-Process," I rolled my eyes and thought this is just another consulting model for explaining the obvious.

It's easy...you assess where you are, plan where you want to go, then decide how you're going to get there. Big deal, I thought. It's basically the same as every other engineering or improvement model.

After my hissy fit, I began to realize that this formula is way more powerful than I first thought. Everywhere I looked, no matter the field or application, it reveals the basic process for making things better, including building a data-driven culture. Instead of stressing out by focusing on everything that's going wrong, you just concentrate on three areas:

# Improvement Formula

*Present*

Are you happy with how things are right now? If so, leave them alone. If not, focus on the future.

*Future*

What would you like to have, do or become? This is goal setting 101. And like many things in life, it's easy to do—and even easier not to do. Being specific about where you are going focuses the journey and helps you keep on track. We all need challenging goals. Once you have one, spend the rest of your time working on your process, or how you will get from where you are to where you want to go.

*Process*

This is the secret sauce: The better your process, the better your results. If you're accomplishing your goals and getting the results you want, keep going. If not, focus your energies on improving your process.

## Everyday Examples of the Improvement Formula

Is taking out your kitchen garbage a problem? If it constantly piles up and there always seems to be a screaming match to get it out of the house, you have a problem with your process.

On the other hand, if the garbage goes out almost automatically, then you figured out a system for collecting it, putting it outside and having it hauled away regularly (even if you've delegated it to someone else). You probably also know when to buy more trash bags, where to store your cans, what night you need to move your cans to the curb and how to pay your garbage bill on time.

Why do McDonald's hamburgers taste the same everywhere? Because they figured out a process for how to put the burger on the grill, when to flip it, how to put it on the bun, what ingredients go on top and the best way to wrap up the sandwich--then they wrote it in an operations manual and trained everyone else the right way to make a burger...every time.

I had a friend who got fired from McDonald's for being "creative" while he was making burgers. Instead of putting on the ketchup first, then the mustard and finally the pickle, he got bored and would mix up the steps. Sometimes pickles were first. Other times, it was the mustard. His manager, who was responsible for making sure that the burgers in that store were made the same way as in every other McDonald's, didn't care for my friend's "new process" and got rid of him.

## Applying the Improvement Formula

Now, imagine what happens if you start to think of your company, marketing, design or any other task or important item in your life using these same three buckets.

If things could be better (Present) and you have an idea of what you'd like them to be (Future), then start working on what you need to do to reach your goal (Process). If you're like me, the process will take the most effort and time, so get to it as quickly as you can.

Certainly, data can help you better manage the entire process by more clearly figuring out where you are right now, planning where you'd like to be and, most importantly, starting, managing and improving the process you're using to get from where you are to where you want to go.

As you might expect, the improvement process is endless. Today's present was yesterday's future. Once you see improvements, be patient. You're probably going to have to repeat these three steps a lot to continue making refinements until you feel like things are really humming.

So, this model gives a good overview of just about everything you're trying to do as you establish and build a data-driven culture. And you may eventually find, like I did, that this Present-Future-Process concept really is THE BIG DEAL!

# STEP 3

# REALIZE YOU'RE FIGHING A BATTLE OF PERCEPTIONS

People have choices. They can buy or not buy your products and services. They can believe or not believe what you say. They can make or break you.

Life is a battle of perceptions, not people. Something is true, if enough people believe it's true. This isn't a joke. It's the "rhetorical" definition of truth and matters greatly in many aspects of life and business.

Once you realize that just about everything in your life is a battle of perceptions (what people think, how much they agree with you, whether they want your product), it becomes obvious why you would want a data-driven culture.

People are persuadable. Facts, information, examples of something that happened to a real person (like customers, suppliers, competitors), quantification and so much more are almost always more persuasive than hunches, guesswork, general beliefs and made up stories.

Some years ago, the Pittsburgh Pirates asked me to help them test potential team logos, so we brought in about 75 people who typically wear sports apparel—elementary, middle and high school students—to comment on various designs.

Based on their input, Major League Baseball created this logo (note the lettering, cross bats instead of cross bones, black polka dot bandana instead of a white one, earring, eyepatch, shaved beard and growl—all separate elements from different logos built into the final version).

## Composite Logo Built from Best Parts[1]

Not only was it a great logo, it became the number one merchandise seller in all of Major League Baseball the year it was introduced. That's a home run, especially when you consider that management thought a skull with an eyepatch would be the best logo. It was not, because it scared the younger kids to death. Instead, the skull with an eyepatch became an alternative logo that teenagers could buy in the gift shop.

---

[1] Used with permission from the Pittsburgh Pirates.

These battles of perceptions are raging both inside and outside your company. How you think about your organization, how well it's running, whether you're reaching your targets, whether your staff or colleagues agree with your assessments, how much support you have for your initiatives—these are all manifestations of how much others believe you.

Not every time, but more often than not, you get them on your side by presenting persuasive data. Generally, the more they agree, the easier time you have moving forward.

Customers, vendors, government officials and every other external stakeholder also operate based on their perceptions and, because they are human, they are persuadable. As with those inside your organization, they tend to favor and believe data over assertions.

## Ancient Model of Persuasion Still Works Great

Not to turn into a professor, but you may remember from a philosophy or rhetoric class in college Aristotle's theory of persuasion that includes ethos, logos and pathos. It's helpful in explaining why a data-driven culture works.

*Ethos*

Ethos is your "personal credibility." If you've been around a long time, have an important title and earned the respect of others, you are more persuasive than the opposite. Data—collected, analyzed and presented effectively—builds ethos.

Most people are not the world's renowned expert in their field, so we can all usually benefit from a coherent presentation of the "facts." I use quotes because I'm using the rhetorical definition of facts or truths which asserts that if enough people believe something to be true, then it's true. (While you may not buy a Chia Pet, enough people do every year that Joseph Enterprises, Inc. can afford TV advertising every holiday season. Or, who would have guessed that consumers would be willing to pay $2 for a bottle of water from a vending machine?)

*Pathos*

Pathos are the "feelings you evoke." Does anyone get excited listening to you or thinking about your ideas? These are often called emotional appeals.

Terrific data insights will fall flat and miss the mark if they are not communicated with some energy in a way that grabs the attention of others. It's not enough to have "data," it has to be communicated in a way that connects with someone's feelings and not only convinces them to believe it, but to act upon it.

*Logos*

Logos is both "logical reasoning" and the "power of the name." Most people will concede that data is more in the logical reasoning camp than guessing or hunches. By using data, you naturally build your logical credibility.

But there's more, because logos is also about the words you use to name what you're talking about. As an example, every organization has good (profit, growth, market share) and bad (recall, shortfall, customer complaint) words. To be more persuasive, find a way to make data-driven a good word and connect your recommendations to words that are positive and likely to persuade your internal and external audiences.

Each of these elements of your credibility can be used to help persuade others to your point of view. Since many situations are "rhetorical" or controversial, this battle of perceptions rages on.

One additional way to think about perceptions is to consider the "weaker" and "stronger" arguments. A weaker argument is believed by fewer people than a stronger argument, and they can flip or change over time. For example, Polaroid cameras used to be the best and everyone wanted one. Enter the digital camera. Before long, no one wanted a Polaroid anymore and digital cameras took over the market because they offered new features and benefits that the Polaroid cameras did not. Then digital cameras died when smartphones started including even better cameras that were easier to operate, store pictures and post on social media. The point is that people's opinions of what's "the best" change as new technologies become available and more people start using one over the alternatives.

In any situation where there are two or more sides, those who have the stronger argument will try to protect and maintain it, while those who have the weaker one will try to get more and more people to believe their side and, if enough eventually do, they will flip and become the stronger argument.

## A Data-driven Culture Is about Persuading Yourself—and Others—to Do Something

In case I wasn't clear (or you missed it), the primary reason for building a data-driven culture is to persuade other people (internal, external and even yourself) to your point of view. Because these people have free will, choices and can think of all different kinds of things, data is a great tool for persuading them.

But just showing them numbers doesn't cut it, they have to be packaged in a way that is based on either your or someone from your staff's personal credibility, bring up feelings in the people you're presenting them to and be based on logical thinking. And, if you can link them to a word or concept to define them, it makes your job of persuading them even easier.

# STEP 4

# BE CLEAR ABOUT WHAT YOU WANT

Most leaders have an idea of what they want to accomplish. But that doesn't mean they know how to communicate it to the people whose job it is to turn those ideas into a reality.

This graphic shows some results from one of my 360 surveys I use to train frontline supervisors and managers to communicate more effectively.

## Top 3 Ways Employees Think
### Managers Can Improve Communication

 Considering my points of view

 Explaining how my job impacts the company's success

 Spelling out the big picture and where we're headed

Survey of 1,970 employees rating 288 managers.
CorCom, Inc. | www.corcom-inc.com

Over half of these employees thought that their manager could do a better job explaining the big picture, by spelling out how their (the employee's) job impacts the success of the company and do a better job considering their (the employee's) point of view. This is true for everything at their job, including building a data-driven culture.

## Fake Goals

What's going on with these employees?

To me, the answer is fairly straight forward. The goals or specifics of what managers want their staff to do are not articulated clearly enough that these employees can be confident in what they need to do.

I call these general, directional statements "fake goals." Here's some examples:

- To grow the business.
- To improve our brand image.
- To increase efficiency.
- To serve customers better.

It's nice that you want to accomplish this, but written and thought about this way, how would you ever know if someone was making progress? There's too much wiggle room. What, exactly, are you talking about or trying to accomplish?

Because they are vague, include no quantification and have no deadline, they tend to breed confusion, inaction and guessing. They cause people to spin their wheels, waste time and work on the wrong stuff.

They can be made a lot better by adding some more details and turning them into real goals, such as:

- To grow the business by 5% by the end of this fiscal year.

- To improve our brand image among female consumers by 2% as measured by our annual tracking survey.

- To increase the efficiency of our southern plant production line by 10 units per hour.

- To serve customers better and consistently receive a 98% positive rating on our ongoing customer satisfaction survey.

You get the idea. When you go from general to specific, it clears up a lot of the problems you're likely to have later.

So, the first question to ask yourself is whether you're setting fake or real goals with respect to the data-driven decisions you'd like to see. Making sure that the goals are specific makes deciding what data to collect, how to measure it and what to conclude about it a whole lot easier.

**Vague Research Questions Waste Time**

A second obstacle to creating a data-driven culture or finding the information you need to make more disciplined decisions are vague questions.

Questions are helpful in defining, understanding and analyzing problems. But vague questions are not helpful, because people tend to wander all over the place and waste a lot of time.

When I was in graduate school, my favorite professor, Don Egolf, would always say, "Knowing the question is knowing half of the answer." Boy, was he right. What you decide to focus upon starts your thinking. And stating those research questions as specifically as possible makes finding the answer a lot easier. Consider these example questions and their potential impact on the analysis that might follow:

- How can we reduce our scrap from 1% to .001%?

- What are customers thinking about in the five minutes before they finally decide to make a buying decision? What can we do to better influence those thoughts?

- If we can convince 5% more of the prospects who contact us to request a bid, what would that do to our overall sales?

- If we can raise our customer satisfaction scores by 3%, how does that translate into the lifetime value of a customer (total amount of sales based on the entire life of a single customer)?

Start with the end in mind. Before you gather information, make sure that you have specific goals or are asking concrete questions. Doing either or both will make your life much easier and everything else better.

# STEP 5

# USE ADDITION, ACCOUNTING AND ATTITUDE MEASURES

Qualitative data, like the kinds of insights you get from talking to someone one-on-one, attending a focus group or reading comments online, are certainly helpful, but "words" are not as persuasive as "numbers."

I like to think of the data you're going to collect as coming from three buckets or types of information I call the three "As":

*Addition*

These are any numbers that you can count, typically from customer records, time trials, visits to a website, number of complaints and others. With most of these, the more there are of a specific number, the more significant the issue.

*Accounting*

These measures, of course, have everything to do with money. They can be dollars or any descriptions of dollars, such as terms like profit, price, purchase amount, net present value, breakeven and many others.

*Attitude*

These measures attempt to understand someone's perceptions and are typically gathered through marketing research where someone describes what they think through surveys, experiments, direct observations and many other techniques.

When you're trying to accomplish a concrete goal, or answer a specific research question, search for one of these three types of data or some combination of them.

## Begin with What You Already Have or Know

As a rule of thumb, it's usually easier to start with what you know or what you might already have, like historical financial data, customer logs, proposals and any other existing data sources.

Unfortunately, many organizations have dysfunctional teams. They don't use a common language or terminology to discuss the business. They have their own goals and associated timing, which may not be connected to the overall business. Some use partial operating information and financial data. In other words, problems are common and they can easily become obstacles to what otherwise seem like sensible inquiries.

If your organization isn't divided into silos (and hopefully not fiefdoms that don't cooperate with each other, like IT taking weeks to run simple reports, or research departments that are too busy with other projects to help you), this data can be highly valuable. Take a look at it first before you decide to invest time and money into getting something that you don't already have.

Some years ago, a local hospital decided to close its emergency room and noticed that its patient census dropped off dramatically. The first thought was to run a survey of community residents to determine if they knew the hospital was still open and they could still come there to get treatment, but NOT for emergencies like a heart attack.

Before running a survey, I suggested looking at who's coming to the hospital. Was the drop off across the board or did certain groups stop coming?

The hospital staff did their own analysis and quickly found that mostly non-insured patients were the ones who were no longer coming. These were the people who were using the emergency room as their doctor's office.

The hospital decided it didn't need to run a community survey because it was able to learn what was going on with data it had already collect.

## Words vs. Numbers

While there are dozens of ways you can collect data, most primary research falls into two broad categories:

### 1. *Qualitative*

These would include focus groups and one-on-one

interviews. They are considered qualitative, because they often include open-ended questions (or words) that ask people to explain what they are thinking or experiencing in detail. Since they are not completely scripted, they can give you opportunities to ask follow-up questions and explore what you're learning as you go along.

Certainly, words can be counted and analyzed, which is growing with the explosion of social media, blogs and live streaming. Summarizing this kind of data can help quickly articulate trends and insights into your data.

How often something is talked about can also be insightful. A search of the American Standard Bible for the terms "heaven" and "hell" in the Gospels turns up something interesting based on the number of mentions: Heaven, 147; hell: 12. Based on this count, heaven was mentioned over ten times more than hell.

## 2. *Quantitative*

These include online surveys, phone polls, automated polls, intercept interviews, experiments and the like. Since they are primarily about the numbers, the questions can be more structured and you usually end up talking with more people than in qualitative studies.

Years ago, when I first started selling marketing research, I spent a lot of time explaining to people why a survey was important and how customer feedback could help them grow their organization. Boy, have things changed. Now, I get questions like, "What's the margin of error on this project?" Which, of course, is a much more sophisticated and nuanced question.

## Words and Numbers

The most valuable insights often come from a combination of sources and data, including qualitative and quantitative.

Even within the same primary survey, asking a few open-ended questions can give you insights that ratings, laundry lists and other forced choice questions never do. So, keep an open mind and focus more on what you want to learn—and what you want to do with the information you want to learn—as you are deciding which tool is best for your situation.

Lloyd Corder, Ph.D.

# STEP 6

# SETUP YOUR DATA CORRECTLY IN A SPREADSHEET YOU CAN ANALYZE

It never ceases to amaze me how many people—even ones who are good at analyzing information—don't know how to setup a spreadsheet. If someone's having problems analyzing their data, it can usually be traced back to how they set up their data.

A spreadsheet forces you to take the first step in organizing your data systematically so you can later analyze it. Generally, the more organized your spreadsheet, the easier your analysis. Spreadsheets that have data all over the place, descriptions that no one else understands (or that you'll never remember two weeks from now) and other general sloppiness just make your job more difficult.

This is what a basic spreadsheet might look like for data about college students with the variables in each column (age, gender, major, ethnicity and GPA) and individual records, observations or people's responses in the rows (different students).

# Structure of a Simple Data File

| Age | Gender | Major | Ethnicity | GPA |
|-----|--------|---------------|-----------|-----|
| 23  | M      | Finance       | WH        | 3.9 |
| 21  | F      | Marketing     | WH        | 3.2 |
| 21  | M      | Accounting    | AA        | 3.6 |
| 22  | M      | Communication | WH        | 2.8 |
| 20  | F      | Accounting    | AS        | 3.7 |
| 22  | F      | Marketing     | AS        | 3.5 |
| 25  | F      | Marketing     | AA        | 3.9 |
| 21  | M      | Finance       | HIS       | 4.0 |
| 22  | F      | Communication | NA        | 2.6 |
| 20  | M      | Economics     | NA        | 2.3 |
| 24  | F      | Economics     | WH        | 3.3 |
| 22  | F      | Finance       | WH        | 3.7 |
| 23  | F      | Finance       | AA        | 3.1 |
| 20  | M      | Economics     | AA        | 2.8 |
| 21  | M      | Communication | AS        | 3.6 |
| 21  | F      | Marketing     | WH        | 3.4 |
| 21  | F      | Finance       | WH        | 2.6 |
| 22  | M      | Marketing     | HIS       | 3.1 |
| 22  | F      | Marketing     | AS        | 3.8 |
| 25  | M      | Communication | AS        | 3.9 |

Note some of the important elements of this file:

*One Variable = One Column*

Individual variables are listed at the top of each column. To analyze something easily, it's best if single variables are contained within individual columns.

What you don't see in this file are combination variables such as gender and major in the same column. When specific types of data are listed in single columns, you can count how many times they occur, as well as crosstab (or compare) it to any number of other variables you might have with that data (GPA by gender).

*One Person/Group of Data = One Row*

Each row represents a different person or observation. Let's say you have someone who filled out a survey by answering the five questions. Each line would be a different person with their answers to each of the five questions.

*Numbers and Words in the Same Column Can Cause Problems*

Depending upon your computer program, it may not be possible to analyze data within a column where some items are numbers and others are words. This usually isn't a problem if you're building pivot tables in Excel (look this up online for various examples of how to use this function).

One of my clients asked me to come in and look at one of their data files that they used to track the installation of over 30,000 desktops. They couldn't figure out how to analyze it. After a minute of showing it to me, I suggested they take the columns that had a mix of words and numbers and make them one or the other. The meeting ended after five minutes, because that solved the problem.

*All Data Files Need Cleaning*

Few data files are perfect, so learning how to handle missing data, inaccurate responses and any host of other issues will need to be addressed as you "clean" the data.

Be very careful here that you don't slant what you've found and make up conclusions based on your cleaning vs.

actual findings. But, it is very rare that you get a data file that doesn't have some missing data, problems or other issues that need addressed before and while you're analyzing it.

## *Most Spreadsheets Have Built-in Analysis Tools*

Once your data file is set up, you can start drawing conclusions quickly.

Most computers have Excel or access to Google Sheets and both include several built-in tools, like how many records you have or the average score for an individual row you've highlighted. Also, they typically list the minimum and maximum values in each row. Finally, most can be quickly customized to report the kinds of statistics you use most.

In Excel, for example, if you highlight all the data in your table and click "Control T" (or "Command T" if you're using a Mac), it creates a table that has dropdown menus at the top of each row. You can click each dropdown menu (right top corner of the cell at the top of each column) and then select any combination of different responses within each cell by selecting or unselecting the responses you want. By highlighting the cells that are left, you can quickly summarize by hand, sort and gather any number of other insights.

Spending a few minutes learning the basics of these programs can help you do a lot of the simple analysis you might need in most situations. Once you and your people get comfortable, they might not even need to go to more advanced programs to find what you need.

These same tools, especially Excel, can help you generate a number of graphs and charts that can be quickly and easily customized. Once I get a chart setup and designed the way I like (and that I think I'll use again), I save it as a template, which saves a lot of time building the second similar chart.

Rarely do you need to do a full analysis to find valuable insights. Setup your file correctly and get started.

# STEP 7

# KEEP YOUR FINDINGS SIMPLE, VERY SIMPLE

After all your hard work of gathering and analyzing your data, if you can't summarize what you found in a couple sentences or present it in a simple graph, you're lost.

Most people have to share what they found with others—and some of those people are senior managers. These are the four things they typically want:

## 1. *KISS*

First, they want simple summaries of your conclusions and insights. Executives are smart, but once you get past percentages and means, you lose most people. Plus, the most significant studies are often proved with the simplest of statistics, because they are based on very tight research questions.

## 2. *Accuracy*

Second, they want quick, accurate answers to any questions they have. Beyond your ethos, pathos and logos (Step 2), there's the level of credibility you have before, during and after your meeting.

People will always make decisions about what you're presenting to them, even if it has nothing to do with your data (but more with how you presented it, answered questions, handled pushback and other issues).

## 3. *Confident in You—and Your Numbers*

Third, they want to feel confidence that you looked at the right information and you did your analysis effectively.

Be prepared to quickly show your analysis or answer specific questions on the fly, but not if you're worried they won't be accurate.

Your findings and information is a lot like a "baby," once it comes into the world, it has a life all its own. Trying to take back information you made a mistake on is almost impossible.

## 4. *What You Think*

Finally, some care about your recommendations, others don't.

Depending upon who's in your meeting and what role you're playing, you may be asked to provide what you've seen.

Since I work with a number of companies and industries, I'm often asked what I think compared to what other companies in similar situations are doing. Of course, I don't talk about confidential information, but general themes and trends can be very helpful to my clients.

Offer your recommendations with some humility. No

one likes a showoff or an outsider that is there to dump on an organization, then take off to let them figure how to fix everything by themselves.

**Use Bar Charts (Or Lines) to Show Trends**

Graphs help people visualize the significance of information, but pick the right ones that most clearly communicate what you're trying to show. There are a number of excellent books and guides on this topic. Here's quick example of what I'm talking about. Instead of presenting these two pie charts, try using a side-by-side bar chart to more clearly communicate the differences.

## Pie Charts vs. Bars to Show Trends

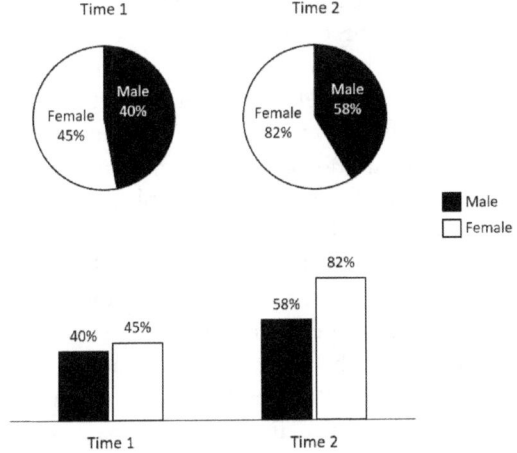

The pie charts don't work with this data, because the percentages don't total 100, although the program picked up the mistake and tried to correct it. The bar charts show a more dramatic change between Time 1 and 2, with the percentage of women increasing faster than did the percentage of men.

## Use Visual Process Models to Focus Perceptions

Another excellent technique, but not necessarily easy to do, is to diagram your findings or conclusions by creating a visual process model. If you're a really strong presenter, you might try using this instead of putting together a PowerPoint or other presentation document. These can be game changing presentations that are much more engaging that others.

You can find plenty of examples of visual process models within presentation and graphics programs and some companies have prebuilt templates you can customize. However, I've always found the best ones are the ones that are completely unique to your situation and that you design for a one time use.

Some years ago, two competing hospital systems located in same small town decided to merge so that they could survive. At first, they didn't do a very good job of communicating why they needed to consolidate and the townsfolk were extremely upset, blaming the managers for the change because they wanted to make more profit and not serve the health care needs of the local community.

I ran several focus groups, employee interviews and surveys, all of which I presented to senior management. At the end of the meeting, I showed this graphic to summarize their situation, which I had thought up during a rather dry sermon at church one day dreaming about Star War's Luke Skywalker being crushed in a trash compacter.

The idea behind this graphic was that the two hospital systems couldn't survive in the same space and they had already started to merge, hence the overlap of the concentric circles.

Using an old rhetorical strategy that says if you want to create a revolution, put the enemy "inside your camp" (which is what was going on, because the executives had become the enemy and bad guys). If you want to get people to unite, put the enemy "outside your camp." The real enemies were competitors, an aging population, government regulations and lower reimbursements from insurance companies—all insights we found in the focus groups and surveys.

## Model for Hospital Merger Challenge

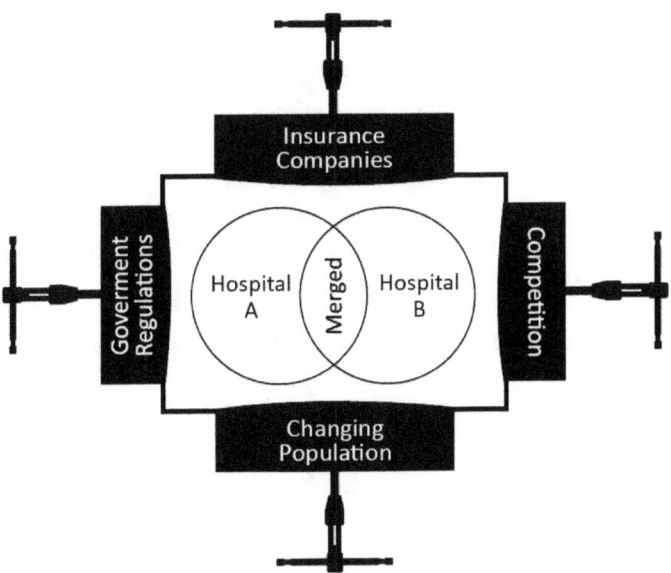

Within a couple of seconds, the executives got it. They understood instantly that what they needed to do was start using messaging about the "external enemies" to better explain why they were actually the good guys, saving the health system.

It worked. Not only did the health system successfully merge, my model helped sell a $500,000 public relations program, which is a big, big project.

## Build a Topline Report Before Diving Deeper

When summarizing and presenting specific data, beginners have a tendency to dive into the specifics and nuances before giving an overview of why they are there and the big picture. It's even more pronounced when there are several people attending the meeting, all with different perspectives, backgrounds and awareness of the issue at hand.

One of the best ways for you to figure out what your analysis shows—and to help others understand what you found—is to prepare a topline report or a broad overview of what you learned. Topline reports can take many forms, ranging from an executive summary to a dashboard. Here's what the student data from Step 6 might look like in a dashboard.

# Topline/Dashboard of Student Data

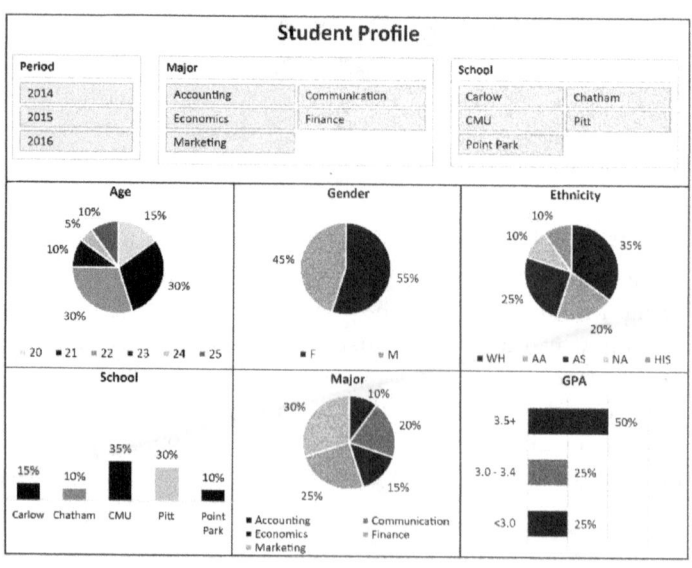

This dashboard was built in Excel. In one page, the total percentage of each variable in the spreadsheet is summarized. Someone could quickly review it to get a sense of what's in the data. Also, in this particular file, there are slicers listed at the top, which would allow the reader to select subsets of the data. These are especially useful if you have a larger data file and want to see if there are differences between any of the groups, such as how the profiles of men and women with respect to this data might be different from one another.

This rule of thumb (present the big picture before any various subcategories or differences) is also helpful in preparing your final data summary or presentation. It's easier for most people to follow someone moving from general to specific points, but not randomly moving all over the place.

Lloyd Corder, Ph.D.

# STEP 8

# ANALYZE YOUR AUDIENCE

Obviously, it's important to think about your audience when putting together your data presentation and findings. After all, these are the people you need to persuade and knowing enough about them is key.

Ask yourself, who's going to be looking at my findings? Before you start the writing process, think about who's going to be listening to you—both in the room, on the phone and looking at what you've come up with long after you finished presenting. These 15 questions can help you get started:

*1. How much do they already know?*

Think about whether your audience has some background in your topic, product or service. If they do, your presentation will be different than if they don't.

## 2. Will they get it?

Is your topic too complex for the audience to understand? If so, what can you do to simplify it? Think of ways you might explain it using analogies, visuals or other examples to a non-technical audience.

## 3. Have they been there?

Does your audience have first-hand experience with the topic? If not, how can I make it more applicable to them?

## 4. Will they evaluate?

Are they likely to evaluate the evidence and examples you use? Do you need to be ready to cite sources or provide other facts? Do you need to have backup data ready from your analysis that you can quickly reference (and not let the meeting get off track)?

## 5. Is it focused?

Is my topic tangled up with other difficult topics? If so, you may need to simplify the plan and focus on just one or a few of these.

## 6. Will it keep their attention?

Is your elevator presentation familiar and boring? If so, what can you do to give it a fresh and exciting perspective? If it's more interesting or presented in a different way, they will be more focused on listening.

## 7. Do they like your topic?

Does the audience have negative, preconceived ideas about

your topic? If so, how can you adjust your presentation to address them or change their minds? In these situations, some speakers use a "sandwich" technique to present negative information in the middle of the presentation, before ending on a more positive note.

*8. Is the topic controversial?*

Will the topic conflict with their beliefs, attitudes and values? If so, are they likely to react to "what you are saying" or "how they are feeling about what you are saying?"

*9. What will they need to do?*

How much time, money and effort are required for your audience to do what you're suggesting? Are you suggesting a major change, investment or some other course of action? Will you want/need a decision on that in your meeting?

*10. What do the leaders think?*

If you're speaking to a group, what do the formal and informal leaders think about the topic? If you win over the top boss in your meeting, will others follow along?

*11. Will they run into resistance from others if they agree with your analysis and recommendations?*

If they do what you want, how much resistance can they expect from friends, family and peers.

*12. Is this the right audience?*

Can you reach the people you want to persuade at the meeting, or is this a step along the way? Are you presenting to the true decision-makers?

*13. Who needs to buy in?*

Will the people at your meeting have to work together to accomplish what you want or will they have to work alone? Are they motivated to do this?

*14. What's the complexity level of what you're asking?*

Is what you want them to do simple, obvious and likely to produce immediate rewards, or is it complex and difficult to evaluate?

*15. What will they think?*

How are they likely to interpret what you have to say?

# STEP 9

# TELL A STORY TO MAKE YOUR DATA MORE INTERESTING AND USABLE

Stories captivate people of all ages. *Where the Wild Things Are*, *Goodnight Moon* and *Cat in the Hat* are all childhood classics. You can probably still remember your favorite bedtime story as a kid.

Storytelling is often thought of as a pastime. However, it is also a strong tool in the business world that is continuing to gain power. Telling a story about your data and what you found will make everything go a lot better.

Using this method allows you as a speaker to reach your audience in ways that are not otherwise possible. By ditching the typical conference routine, your audience will be more likely to follow along with what you're saying during your meeting and recall what you said later.

There are two parts to every good story: the storyline and the storyteller. Both have certain criteria that must be met in order to be interesting and compelling.

## Part One: The Storyline

Let's start with the storyline, because it's important to have something interesting to say.

There are five basic parts of most storylines that should be considered as you decide how to talk about your data, findings and recommendations.

*1. Relatable Characters*

You must deliver the story in a way that is relatable to the audience. You want your audience to be able to put themselves in the shoes of at least one character in the story to empathize with the plot. If your audience can recall a situation when they felt or acted similarly to a character, they are more likely to maintain interest and agreement.

Is there a customer, prospect, employee or someone else who has experienced what you're talking about? Is there someone in the room who's likely to have firsthand experience? If so, these could be good sources for finding a relatable character.

Remember to include a few visuals when describing your characters. Instead of, "Sally is a customer," you might try, "Sally, one of our customers, is about 40 years old, tall and has red hair." A few minor visuals can help paint a picture that others will envision in their mind.

*2. Clear Setting*

The time and place of your story should be clear to set the background. When your audience can envision the setting in their mind, it becomes more real. This way they will have greater attention and understanding of the situation.

What led you to this point? What was happening or not happening? Would summarizing how this fits into the Improvement Formula (presented earlier in Step 2) help set the stage?

## 3. Plot

The main incident or series of small events that the characters are involved in is the plot. These events and character responses all relate back to the main conflict of the story as a whole. The plot is the overall story such as a tale of success, revenge, tragedy, etc.

What was going on with your characters? What's the issue? What's the benefit of solving the problem or capitalizing upon the opportunity?

## 4. Conflict

The conflict is the main issue that drives your story. The conflict can be between two characters, one character and an event, or even a single character battling something within themselves. Make the conflict a common issue that most people face in order to make it more applicable.

Remember, when there's a conflict there are two or more sides to an issue. What are the "weaker" and "stronger" arguments (sides believed by the fewest/most people)? How critical is it to resolve the conflict? What happens if it isn't resolved?

## 5. Main Theme

This is the central idea that you are presenting to your audience throughout the entirety of the story. The main takeaway from your story is a result of the main theme—and the reason that most presentations move from the "general" to the "specific" in terms of the insights.

Saying your theme one time usually isn't enough. You may have to refer to it in the beginning, throughout out and during your summary.

Ask yourself a basic question, "If my audience walks away with only one idea, what should it be?" That is your main theme. Everything else in your presentation is about supporting that theme with examples, graphs, statistics and whatever else you've prepared.

## Part Two: The Storyteller

Once you have a storyline, your story needs to be told in an impactful way. "How you say it," matters, perhaps as much or more than what you're actually saying. There are four essential tasks.

*1. Keep Their Attention*

You must capture your audience's attention within the first few seconds. Most people's attention spans are short, especially in our present lives where we've trained ourselves to be distracted by social media, email, texts, calls and numerous other interruptions.

Create a strong opening that demands the attention of your audience right from the beginning to limit other distractions that could take away from the effectiveness of your story.

Can you state a fact? Show an interesting statistic? Refer to a historic event? Tell a joke (if you're good at telling jokes and are positive it won't offend someone in your audience)? Have someone introduce your topic and/or you? Show an interesting graphic or picture? These are just a few of many ways you can help get your listeners attention—and help them start thinking about what you have to say instead of what they were focused on five minutes ago.

*2. Play on Emotions*

The emotion that you are aiming to channel will vary with

each story and objective, but be sure to focus heavily on the sentiment of your audience. This connection will make your story seem less like a lecture or speech and more like a genuine conversation with the people in the room.

When they can relate both mentally and emotionally to your subject, they are more likely to go along with your ideas. Although logic plays a big part in decision making, emotions are also a major factor. Make the most of your meeting by incorporating both logic and emotion.

One of the best ways to do this is to speak extemporaneously, from notes, not reading, memorization or impromptu. Be prepared in what you have to say, but flexible enough that you can adjust as you move through your meeting. Presenting from notes sounds much more natural and credible than other delivery formats.

*3. Alter Your Tone of Voice*

Recall your bedtime stories as a child. Did your parents read in the same voice throughout the entire book? Most likely the answer is no.

The bottom line is that no one wants to listen to a monotone speaker, regardless of their age. Capture each emotion and important detail by fluctuating the speed, tone and volume of your voice.

This is a particular problem for technical speakers and those who are speaking English as a second language. Because some of these speakers get nervous, they talk fast. When someone has trouble understanding your terminology or accent, listening becomes extremely difficult and some people just give up.

The solution to these challenges is to simply explain the technical information or challenge and, for non-native English speakers, slow down and over articulate your words. Just like the makeup put on a stage actor that looks ridiculous when off stage, under the bright lights it seems natural.

Speaking a little slower, louder or other adjustments will seem strange to the presenter, but natural to the audience.

## 4. Incorporate Movement

Hand gestures should correspond to what you are saying. If possible, stand up and move around the room to maintain the interest of your audience.

If someone seems to be shifting the focus of your meeting, move closer to this person to bring them back to your story. However, be careful not to become a distraction by moving too fast or frequently.

Use hand gestures and facial expressions with a purpose to emphasize your point, not take away from it.

Finally, consider "anchoring" the room to make opposing points. For example, maybe stand on the right side of the room to make positive points about your topic, then walk to the left side to make the negative points. Most times, your audience won't realize you're doing this, but nonverbally it helps them correspond specific types of ideas to where you are standing.

By capturing your audience's focus from the beginning, retaining their attention throughout the meeting and staying in their memory afterwards, your company will benefit the most.

Whether you are pitching the results of your data to coworkers, current clients or potential customers, a single story can go a long way. So, forget the notion that storytelling is for children and leisurely activities. Some things people just don't grow out of. The love of a good story is one of them.

# STEP 10

# USE A SNOWMAN TO ORGANIZE YOUR MEETING

We've all be in painful meetings that waste everyone's time. Promise yourself not to continue this trend when you're presenting your data-driven insights and recommendations. A data-driven culture should be something positive for the organizations who use it, not something people roll their eyes about every time they hear it.

## The Inverted Snowman

One of the reasons some meetings are so boring and ineffective is because they are organized in what my friend, Jerry McNellis, called the "inverted snowman." Typical meetings spend a lot of time on information, updates and reports, then less time on making actual decisions and rarely anytime on strategic thinking.

As this graph shows, the larger the circle, the more time spent on that part of the meeting. With the inverted snowman, almost no time is spent on strategic thinking.

# The Inverted Snowman

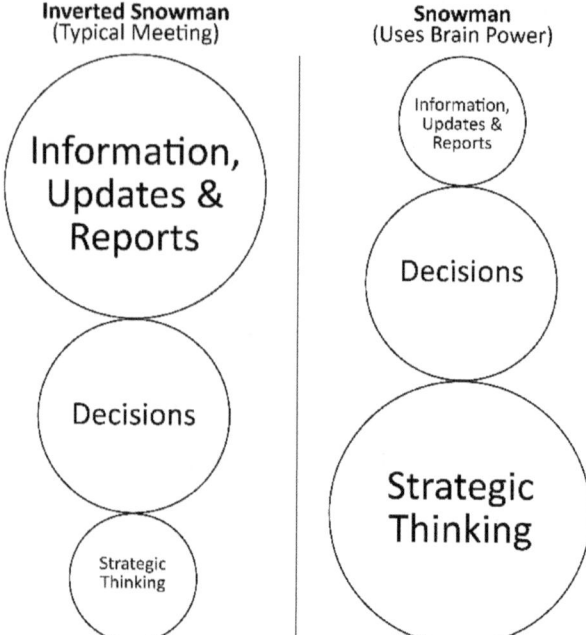

Ironically, this is the exact opposite of how most executives want to spend their time. They tend to want a quick overview of the information that they can understand, then it's decision-making time or time to think strategically about what to do next.

So, why not restructure your meetings so you can grab more of the brainpower of the people in the room and spend less time regurgitating information? Why would you invest in any type of data analysis and presentation without making a decision about how you're going to use it?

Moreover, what are the strategic implications of the data that you've found and presented?

## Meeting Checklist

As you're deciding if and how you might organize your meeting using the snowman organizational format, don't forget these important questions to help ensure your meeting stays on track:

- Do you really need a meeting?

- Do we have a clear objective and agenda?

- Screens down/off?

- How will I keep someone from monopolizing or dominating my meeting? What problem personalities might be in attendance?

- Can I manage the seating arrangements? I like to sit next to the person I have to persuade during the meeting. If you're across the table (and if you're entire team is on the same side of the table), it has the potential to create unnecessary conflict that can be avoided if everyone sits in a mixed up pattern or if you sit at a 90 or 45 degree angle from the person you have to persuade.

- Do we need introductions or name cards? Does everyone know everyone?

- What can we do to NOT waste time?

- Will we start and end on time?

- How can we move quickly through the meeting and keep it interesting?

- Will I and other presenters be able to stand up when we're speaking? Remember, by standing up you naturally take control of the room and have more power than when you're sitting down. Even if you move between sitting and standing, you gain a slight advantage.

- At the end of the meeting, agree on who's doing what, by when. If we're not making important decisions or thinking strategically about our situation, why are we having a meeting?

While a lot of people think holding a meeting is obvious and doesn't require that much thought, it actually does, especially when it's going to be a key part of building and sustaining a data-driven culture. Why not make every second count?

## *Summary of* SMART DATA: 10 SIMPLE STEPS FOR MAKING BETTER, FASTER BUSINESS DECISIONS

*Step 1: Start with Your People, Not Your System*

Everyone has mix of technical and soft skills that can both be improved when you adopt a data-driven management philosophy. Create an environment where your people gather, analyze and present data to help make important decisions.

*Step 2: Simplify Your Opportunities by Using the Improvement Formula*

Memorize it: Present-Future-Process. Evaluate where you are, decide where you want to go, spend the rest of your time figuring out how to get there. This formula works for explaining almost everything within your organization and will help simplify problems, challenges and opportunities so that you can use a data-driven approach to improve them.

*Step 3: Realize You're Fighting a Battle of Perceptions*

What's in other people's heads matters most, especially if you need their help to be successful. They have free will and can think whatever they want. However, they are often persuaded by data, especially carefully crafted, analyzed and presented information.

*Step 4: Be Clear about What You Want*

Don't waste time by offering little to no direction about what you want or need from your data requests. Be specific—with your goals and questions—so you can get better results without everyone spinning their wheels.

## *Step 5: Use Addition, Accounting and Attitude Measures*

Those are the three big buckets of data you can use in your analyses. They are things you can count, money and survey ratings.

## *Step 6: Setup Your Data Correctly in a Spreadsheet You Can Analyze*

Individual variables (or topics) go in the columns. Individual responses or sets of information go in the rows. A systematic, disciplined approach will make your analysis a lot easier and more accurate. Don't forget, most spreadsheets already have a number of valuable tools in them that you may be able to use to analyze a lot of the information you collect.

## *Step 7: Keep Your Findings Simple, Very Simple*

While you might spend a month collecting and analyzing your data, being able to summarize what you found in one sentence should be the goal. Group your findings into 2-3 main themes that others can quickly grasp and use.

## *Step 8: Analyze Your Audience*

Avoid going in blind. Find out who needs the summary of your findings, what they already know, what biases they might have and the like. Taking time to prepare and adapt your results will save you frustration and heartache during and after you present what you found.

*Step 9: Tell an Interesting Story*

Almost everyone loves a good story, especially when it makes your data and findings more interesting, relevant and useful. Use the elements of an effective story to describe what you plan to say.

*Step 10: Use a Snowman to Organize Your Meeting*

Most meetings waste a lot of time on presenting information and talking "at" the participants. Flip it around and spend less time doing this and more time getting decisions on your data has found and strategic input—the kind of information other executives like to focus on.

Lloyd Corder, Ph.D.

# LLOYD CORDER, PH.D.

Lloyd Corder, Ph.D., is founder and CEO of strategic marketing research firm CorCom, Inc. and teaches at Tepper School of Business at Carnegie Mellon University and the University of Pittsburgh.

He is a frequent keynote, convention and motivational speaker, and he has appeared on business-oriented radio and television programs. Corder's studies have been published in more than 500 magazines and newspapers.

Recent books, free resources and other helpful materials are available at CorCom, Inc.'s website or directly from the company. You can also order this and other printed books or Kindle downloads from Amazon (www.amazon.com).

CorCom, Inc.
www.corcom-inc.com
info@corcom-inc.com
412.201.2636

Lloyd Corder, Ph.D.

www.ingramcontent.com/pod-product-compliance
Lightning Source LLC
Chambersburg PA
CBHW061201180526
45170CB00002B/909